The Story of
Passover

The Story of
Passover

GRAMERCY BOOKS
• New York •

Preface and compilation
copyright © 2000 by Random House Value Publishing, Inc.
All rights reserved under International and Pan-American
Copyright Conventions.

No part of this book may be reproduced or transmitted in any form
or by any means electronic or mechanical including photocopying,
recording, or by any information storage and retrieval system,
without permission in writing from the publisher.

This 2000 edition is published by Gramercy Books™,
an imprint of Random House Value Publishing, Inc.,
201 East 50th Street, New York, New York 10022.

Gramercy Books™ and colophon are trademarks of
Random House Value Publishing, Inc.

Random House
New York • Toronto • London • Sydney • Auckland

Printed and bound in Singapore

Compiled, edited, designed, and composited by
Frank J. Finamore

A CIP catalog record for this book is available from the Library of
Congress.

The Story of Passover
ISBN 0–517–19457–0

8   7   6   5   4   3   2   1

✡ Contents ✡

Passover Recipes

✡ PREFACE ✡

Pesah, or Passover, following biblical law, is observed seven days, beginning on the eve of the 15th and ending on the 21st of Nisan. The first and last days are holy days on which divine services are held in the synagogues. The intervening days, known as *Hol Hamoed,* are half-holy days. The holiday celebrates the emancipation of the Jewish people to freedom from the Egyptians. It was an event that was one of the most important events in the history of the Jewish nation, one that defined it and its people ever since. The name *Pesah* means "passing over," or sparing and delivering, referring to when God killed the firstborn of the Egyptians, sparing the Israelites. Its observance came to be interpreted as a memorial of God's appearance as the avenger of Israel's wrongs. It is also a feast in celebration of the birth of Israel as a holy nation and the belief in God's choice of Israel as his chosen people.

And in the centuries that followed, Passover became a holiday of hope, as the Egyptian bondage was followed by the rule of the Romans, and since the Jewish Diaspora, tyranny by countless nations as the *Haggadah* notes: "in many other lands, have we groaned under the burden of affliction and suffered as victims of malice, ignorance and fanaticism." Through the celebration of the Passover festival the Jewish people defied their ever new Pharaohs and Caesars. Its observance was a perennial source of hope, as it declared, "This year we are slaves; next year may we be free men." At the same time, it is a reminder of the true nature of freedom. Freedom is not just a political and civil condition, it is one of the spirit. As much of the history of the Jewish people has been one of the oppressed, Passover also celebrates inner moral and spiritual liberty. For it is only in observance of the Law of God, that one is truly free and lives up to the responsibility of being Jewish.

Celebrating Passover is an essential part of being Jewish. No matter what language or country, it connects the Jewish people in a bond that stretches back into the shadows of history. With each Passover, its celebrants relive the moment of freedom. With each spring, that memory is resurrected as a reminder of what was and what will be. As the great German-Jewish poet Heinrich Heine wrote, God through Moses created a "holy people, a people of God, destined to outlive the centuries, and to serve as a pattern to all other nations, even as a prototype to the whole of mankind."

NATHAN GREEN

New York
2000

From
The Holy Scriptures

*T*hen Moses called for all the elders of Israel, and said unto them: "Draw out, and take you lambs according to your families, and kill the Passover lamb. And ye shall take a bunch of hyssop, and dip it in the blood that is in the basin, and strike the lintel and the two side-posts with the blood that is in the basin; and none of you shall go out of the door of his house until the morning. For the Lord will pass through to smite the Egyptians; and when He seeth the blood upon the lintel, and on the two side-posts, the Lord will pass over the door, and will not suffer the destroyer to come in unto your houses to smite you. And ye shall observe this thing for an ordinance to thee and to thy sons forever. And it shall come to pass, when ye be come to the land which the Lord will give you, according as He hath promised, that ye shall keep this service. And it shall come to pass, when your children shall say unto you: What mean ye by this service? that ye shall say: It is the sacrifice of the Lord's Passover, for that He passed over the houses of the children of Israel in Egypt, when He smote the Egyptians, and delivered our houses. And the people bowed the head and worshipped. And the children of Israel went and did so; as the Lord had commanded Moses and Aaron, so did they.

And it came to pass at midnight, that the Lord smote all the firstborn in the land of Egypt, from the first-born of Pharaoh that sat on his throne unto the first-born of the captive that was in the dungeon; and all the first-born of cattle. And

Pharaoh rose up in the night, he, and all his servants, and all the Egyptians; and there was a great cry in Egypt; for there was not a house where there was not one dead. And he called for Moses and Aaron by night and said: "Rise up, get you forth from among my people, both ye and the children of Israel; and go, serve the Lord, as ye have said. Take both your flocks and your herds, as ye have said, and be gone; and bless me also." And the Egyptians were urgent upon the people, to send them out of the land in haste; for they said: "We are all dead men." And the people took their dough before it was leavened, their kneading-troughs being bound up in their clothes upon their shoulders. And the children of Israel did according to the word of Moses; and they asked of the Egyptians jewels of silver, and jewels of gold, and raiment. And the Lord gave the people favour in the sight of the Egyptians, so that they let them have what they asked. And they despoiled the Egyptians.

And the children of Israel journeyed from Rameses to Succoth, about six hundred thousand men on foot, beside children. And a mixed multitude went up also with them; and flocks, and herds, even very much cattle. And they baked unleavened cakes of the dough which they brought forth out of Egypt, for it was not leavened; because they were thrust out of Egypt, and could not tarry, neither had they prepared for themselves any victual. Now the time that the children of Israel dwelt in Egypt was four hundred and thirty years. And it came to pass at the end of four hundred and thirty years, even the self-

same day it came to pass, that all the host of the Lord went out from the land of Egypt. It was a night of watching unto the Lord for bringing them out from the land of Egypt; this same night is a night of watching unto the Lord for all the children of Israel throughout their generations.

And the Lord said unto Moses and Aaron: "This is the ordinance of the Passover: there shall no alien eat thereof; but every man's servant that is bought for money, when thou hast circumcised him, then shall he eat thereof. A sojourner and a hired servant shall not eat thereof. In one house shall it be eaten; thou shalt not carry forth aught of the flesh abroad out of the house; neither shall ye break a bone thereof. All the congregation of Israel shall keep it. And when a stranger shall sojourn with thee, and will keep the Passover to the Lord, let all his males be circumcised, and then let him come near and keep it; and he shall be as one that is born in the land; but no uncircumcised person shall eat thereof. One law shall be to him that is homeborn, and unto the stranger that sojourneth among you." Thus did all the children of Israel; as the Lord commanded Moses and Aaron, so did they.

And it came to pass the selfsame day that the Lord did bring the children of Israel out of the land of Egypt by their hosts.

EXODUS 12: 21–51

And it came to pass, when Pharaoh had let the people go, that God led them not by the way of the land of the Philistines, although that was near; for God said: "Lest peradventure the people repent when they see war, and they return to Egypt." But God led the people about, by the way of the wilderness by the Red Sea; and the children of Israel went up armed out of the land of Egypt. And Moses took the bones of Joseph with him; for he had straitly sworn the children of Israel, saying: "God will surely remember you; and ye shall carry up my bones away hence with you." And they took their journey from Succoth, and encamped in Etham, in the edge of the wilderness. And the Lord went before them by day in a pillar of cloud, to lead them the way; and by night in a pillar of fire, to give them light; that they might go by day and by night: the pillar of cloud by day, and the pillar of fire by night, departed not from before the people.

And the Lord spoke unto Moses, saying: "Speak unto the children of Israel, that they turn back and encamp before Pi-hahiroth, between Migdol and the sea, before Baal-zephon, over against it shall ye encamp by the sea. And Pharaoh will say of the children of Israel: They are entangled in the land, the wilderness hath shut them in. And I will harden Pharaoh's heart, and he shall follow after them; and I will get Me honour upon Pharaoh, and upon all his host; and the Egyptians shall know that I am the Lord." And they did so. And it was told the king of Egypt that the people were fled; and the heart of

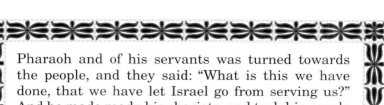

Pharaoh and of his servants was turned towards the people, and they said: "What is this we have done, that we have let Israel go from serving us?" And he made ready his chariots, and took his people with him. And he took six hundred chosen chariots, and all the chariots of Egypt, and captains over all of them. And the Lord hardened the heart of Pharaoh king of Egypt, and he pursued after the children of Israel; for the children of Israel went out with a high hand. And the Egyptians pursued after them, all the horses and chariots of Pharaoh, and his horsemen, and his army, and overtook them encamping by the sea, beside Pi-hahiroth, in front of Baal-zephon. And when Pharaoh drew nigh, the children of Israel lifted up their eyes, and, behold, the Egyptians were marching after them; and they were sore afraid; and the children of Israel cried out unto the Lord. And they said unto Moses: "Because there were no graves in Egypt, hast thou taken us away to die in the wilderness? wherefore hast thou dealt thus with us, to bring us forth out of Egypt? Is not this the word that we spoke unto thee in Egypt, saying: Let us alone, that we may serve the Egyptians? For it were better for us to serve the Egyptians, than that we should die in the wilderness." And Moses said unto the people: "Fear ye not, stand still, and see the salvation of the Lord, which He will work for you today; for whereas ye have seen the Egyptians today, ye shall see them again no more forever. The Lord will fight for you, and ye shall hold your peace."

And the Lord said unto Moses: "Wherefore criest thou unto Me? speak unto the children of Israel, that they go forward. And lift thou up thy rod, and stretch out thy hand over the sea, and divide it; and the children of Israel shall go into the midst of the sea on dry ground. And I, behold, I will harden the hearts of the Egyptians, and they shall go in after them; and I will get Me honour upon Pharaoh, and upon all his host, upon his chariots, and upon his horsemen. And the Egyptians shall know that I am the Lord, when I have gotten Me honour upon Pharaoh, upon his chariots, and upon his horsemen." And the angel of God, who went before the camp of Israel, removed and went behind them; and the pillar of cloud removed from before them, and stood behind them; and it came between the camp of Egypt and the camp of Israel; and there was the cloud and the darkness here, yet gave it light by night there; and the one came not near the other all the night. And Moses stretched out his hand over the sea; and the Lord caused the sea to go back by a strong east wind all the night, and made the sea dry land, and the waters were divided. And the children of Israel went into the midst of the sea upon the dry ground; and the waters were a wall unto them on their right hand, and on their left. And the Egyptians pursued, and went in after them into the midst of the sea, all Pharaoh's horses, his chariots, and his horsemen. And it came to pass in the morning watch, that the Lord looked forth upon the host of the Egyptians through the pillar of fire and of cloud, and discomfited the host of the Egyptians. And He took off their chariot wheels, and made them to drive heavily; so that the Egyptians said: "Let us flee from the face of Israel; for the Lord fighteth for them against the Egyptians."

And the Lord said unto Moses: "Stretch out thy hand over the sea, that the waters may come back upon the Egyptians, upon their chariots, and upon their horsemen." And Moses stretched forth his hand over the sea, and the sea returned to its strength when the morning appeared; and the Egyptians fled against it; and the Lord overthrew the Egyptians in the midst of the sea. And the waters returned, and covered the chariots, and the horsemen, even all the host of Pharaoh that went in after them into the sea; there remained not so much as one of them. But the children of Israel walked upon dry land in the midst of the sea; and the waters were a wall unto them on their right hand, and on their left. Thus the Lord saved Israel that day out of the hand of the Egyptians; and Israel saw the Egyptians dead upon the seashore. And Israel saw the great work which the Lord did upon the Egyptians, and the people feared the Lord; and they believed in the Lord, and in His servant Moses.

Then sang Moses and the children of Israel this song unto the Lord, and spoke, saying:

I will sing unto the Lord, for He is highly exalted;
The horse and his rider hath He thrown into
    the sea.
The Lord is my strength and song,

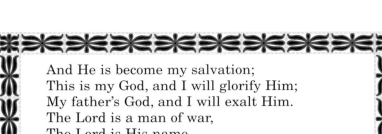

And He is become my salvation;
This is my God, and I will glorify Him;
My father's God, and I will exalt Him.
The Lord is a man of war,
The Lord is His name.
Pharaoh's chariots and his host hath He cast into
    the sea,
And his chosen captains are sunk in the Red Sea.
The deeps cover them—
They went down into the depths like a stone.
Thy right hand, O Lord, glorious in power,
Thy right hand, O Lord, dasheth in pieces the
    enemy.
And in the greatness of Thine excellency Thou
    overthrowest them that rise up against
    Thee;
Thou sendest forth Thy wrath, it consumeth
    them as stubble.
And with the blast of Thy nostrils the waters
    were piled up—
The floods stood upright as a heap;
The deeps were congealed in the heart of the sea.
The enemy said:
"I will pursue, I will overtake, I will divide the
    spoil;
My lust shall be satisfied upon them;
I will draw my sword, my hand shall destroy
    them."
Thou didst blow with Thy wind, the sea covered
    them;
They sank as lead in the mighty waters.

Who is like unto Thee, O Lord, among the
mighty?
Who is like unto Thee, glorious in holiness,
Fearful in praises, doing wonders?
Thou stretchedst out Thy right hand—
The earth swallowed them.
Thou in Thy love hast led the people
that Thou hast redeemed;
Thou hast guided them in Thy strength to
Thy holy habitation.
The peoples have heard, they tremble;
Pangs have taken hold on the inhabitants of
Philistia.
Then were the chiefs of Edom affrighted;
The mighty men of Moab, trembling taketh
hold upon them;
All the inhabitants of Canaan are melted away.
Terror and dread falleth upon them;
By the greatness of Thine arm they are as still
as a stone;
Till Thy people passover, O Lord,
Till the people pass over that Thou
hast gotten.
Thou bringest them in, and plantest them
in the mountain of Thine inheritance,
The place, O Lord, which Thou hast made for
Thee to dwell in,
The sanctuary, O Lord, which Thy hands
have established.
The Lord shall reign forever and ever.
For the horses of Pharaoh went in with his char-

iots and with his horsemen into the sea, and the Lord brought back the waters of the sea upon them; but the children of Israel walked on dry land in the midst of the sea.

And Miriam the prophetess, the sister of Aaron, took a timbrel in her hand; and all the women went out after her with timbrels and with dances. And Miriam sang unto them:

Sing ye to the Lord, for He is highly exalted:

The horse and his rider hath He thrown into the sea.

And Moses led Israel onward from the Red Sea, and they went out into the wilderness of Shur; and they went three days in the wilderness, and found no water. And when they came to Marah, they could not drink of the waters of Marah, for they were bitter. Therefore the name of it was called Marah. And the people murmured against Moses, saying: "What shall we drink?" And he cried unto the Lord; and the Lord showed him a tree, and he cast it into the waters, and the waters were made sweet. There He made for them a statute and an ordinance, and there He proved them; and He said: "If thou wilt diligently hearken to the voice of the Lord thy God, and wilt do that which is right in His eyes, and wilt give ear to His commandments, and keep all His statutes, I will put none of the diseases upon thee, which I have put upon the Egyptians; for I am the Lord that healeth thee."

EXODUS 13: 17–15:26

And in the first month, on the fourteenth day of the month, is the Lord's passover. And on the fifteenth day of this month shall be a feast; seven days shall unleavened bread be eaten. In the first day shall be a holy convocation; ye shall do no manner of servile work; but ye shall present an offering made by fire, a burnt-offering unto the Lord: two young bullocks, and one ram, and seven he-lambs of the first year; they shall be unto you without blemish; and their meal-offering, fine flour mingled with oil; three tenth parts shall ye offer for a bullock, and two tenth parts for the ram; a several tenth part shalt thou offer for every lamb of the seven lambs; and one he-goat for a sin-offering, to make atonement for you. Ye shall offer these beside the burnt-offering of the morning, which is for a continual burnt-offering. After this manner ye shall offer daily, for seven days, the food of the offering made by fire, of a sweet savour unto the Lord; it shall be offered beside the continual burnt-offering, and the drink-offering thereof. And on the seventh day ye shall have a holy convocation; ye shall do no manner of servile work.

NUMBERS 28: 16—25

The Passover
Haggadah

Rites and Symbols of the Seder

The Seder service is marked with special concern for the children. A striking contrast is offered between the ceremonies of this service of the Passover Eve and the conduct of the usual meal, so that the child is sure to ask for an explanation, and thus to give the coveted opportunity to tell the story of Israel's deliverance, and to impress the lesson of faith in God, the Defender of right and the Deliverer of the oppressed. These symbols aim to put us in sympathy with our forefathers of the generation of the Exodus; to feel the trials of their embittered life of bondage and the joy of their subsequent triumph of freedom.

WINE. As in all Jewish ceremonials of rejoicing, such as the welcoming of the Sabbath and the festivals, the solemnizing of marriages, and the naming of a child, so at the Seder, wine is used as a token of festivity. Mead, apple-cider, any fruit juice, or especially unfermented raisin wine, is commonly used at the Seder service.

THE FOUR CUPS. Each participant in the service is expected to drink four cups of wine. This number is determined by the four divine promises of redemption made to Israel in Exodus VI: 6-7: *V'hotzesi, V'hitzalti, V'goalti* and *V'lokahti,* that is, bringing out of bondage, deliverance from servitude, redemption from all dependence in Egypt, and selection as "the people of the Lord." The first cup serves for *Kiddush* as on other holy days and on Sabbath; the second is taken at the conclusion of the first part of the Seder, the third follows the grace after the meal, and the last comes at the end of the second part of the Seder.

THE CUP OF ELIJAH. The fifth promise of God (*V'hevesi*) to bring Israel into Canaan, which follows the four promises of redemption, gave rise to the question of the need of a fifth cup of wine in the Seder. Popular belief left the decision of all mooted questions of law and ritual to the prophet Elijah, the central hero of Jewish legend. The popular mind believed this great champion of righteousness and of pure worship of God to be immortal, and viewed him as the coming forerunner of the Messiah, whose task it will be—among other things—to announce the good tidings of peace and salvation, to effect a union of hearts between parents and their children, to comfort the sorrowing, to raise the dead, and to establish the divine kingdom of righteousness on earth.

The fifth cup, the need of which was left to his decision, came to be known as the Cup of Elijah; and gave rise to the custom of opening the door during the Seder service, that the long expected messenger

of the final redemption of mankind from all oppression might enter the home as a most welcome guest. Our fathers were thus helped, in times of darkness and persecution, to keep in mind the Messianic era of freedom, justice, and goodwill. Stripped of its legendary form, it is still the hope for the realization of which Israel ever yearns and strives.

MATZO. The unleavened bread or the bread of affliction reminds us of the hardships that our fathers endured in Egypt, and of the haste with which they departed thence. Having no time to bake their bread, they had to rely for food upon sun-baked dough which they carried with them.

WATERCRESS or PARSLEY. Either of these greens is suggestive of the customary oriental relish and is used as a token of gratitude to God for the products of the earth. The purpose of dipping it in salt water or vinegar is to make it palatable.

MOROR. The bitter herb—a piece of horseradish—represents the embittered life of the Israelites in Egypt.

HAROSES. This mixture of apples, blanched almonds, and raisins, finely chopped and flavored with cinnamon and wine, was probably originally a condiment. Owing to its appearance, it came to be regarded as representing the clay with which the Israelites made bricks, or the mortar used in the great structures erected by the bondmen of Egypt.

THE ROASTED SHANK-BONE is an emblem of the Paschal lamb.

THE EGG (roasted) is the symbol of the free-will

burnt-offering brought on every day of the feast, during the existence of the Temple in Jerusalem.

APHIKOMON. *Aphikomon* is derived from the Greek, meaning AFTER-MEAL or DESSERT. The origin of this custom must be traced to the Paschal lamb which was eaten on Passover night. It was customary to reserve a small portion of the lamb to be eaten at the close of the meal. When sacrifices had ceased, a piece of the matzo was eaten instead. The *aphikomon,* hidden early in the Seder, is left to the end of the meal, in order that the children may be kept alert during the entire service. In connection with this, a sort of game of paying forfeits originated. The head of the family good-naturedly takes no note of the spiriting away of the *aphikomon* by the children, who do not surrender it until the master of the house is forced to redeem it by some gift, in order that the meal may be concluded.

Directions for Setting the Table

On the table, in front of the person who conducts the service, place a large platter containing Seder symbols:

a. Three matzos each of which is covered separately in the folds of a napkin or special cover. Two of them represent the *Lehem Mishneh*—"double portion"—of the Sabbath and the holy days, and the third the *Lehem 'Oni*—"bread of affliction." These are also taken to represent the three religious divisions of Israel: the "Cohen" (priest), "Levi" (associate priest) and "Yisroel" (lay-Israelite).

b. The roasted shank-bone (of a lamb).

c. A roasted egg.

Also a piece of horseradish, a bit of *haroses,* and a spray of parsley.

Besides these, there are placed on the table for the company:

1. A plate of bitter herbs (horseradish), cut into small pieces.

2. A dish of *haroses*.

3. Parsley or watercress.

4. A dish of salt water.

5. A cup of wine is placed at each plate, and a large brimming goblet in the center of the table for the prophet Elijah.

The meal served during the Seder follows the form of a banquet of olden times. Hence the reference, in the Hebrew texts of the Four Questions, to the custom of reclining on the left side—a position assumed by free men. Preserving this custom, many households still provide a large cushioned armchair for the person conducting the Seder.

The table is usually spread with the best of the family's china and silverware, and adorned with flowers, in keeping with the festive spirit.

Lighting the Festival Lights

To symbolize the joy which the festival brings into the Jewish home, the mistress kindles the lights and recites the following blessing:

Praised art Thou, O Lord our God, King of the universe, who hast sanctified us by Thy commandments, and hast commanded us to kindle the (*on Sabbath add:* Sabbath and) festival lights.

Praised art Thou, O Lord our God, King of the

universe, who hast kept us alive and sustained us and brought us to this season.

May our home be consecrated, O God, by the light of Thy countenance, shining upon us in blessing, and bringing us peace!

Company: Amen.

Kiddush

(On Sabbath eve begin here.)

The master of the house lifts up the wine-cup and says:

Let us praise God and thank Him for all the blessings of the week that is gone; for life, health and strength; for home, love and friendship; for the discipline of our trials and temptations; for the happiness of our success and prosperity. Thou hast ennobled us, O God, by the blessings of work, and in love and grace sanctified us by the blessings of rest, through the commandment, "Six days shalt thou labor and do all thy work, but the seventh day is a Sabbath unto the Lord thy God."

(On weekdays begin here.)

With song and praise, and with the symbols of our feast, let us renew the memories of our past.

Praised art Thou, O Lord our God, King of the

universe, who hast chosen us from all peoples and exalted and sanctified us with Thy commandments. In love hast Thou given us, O Lord our God, solemn days of joy and festive seasons of gladness, even this day of the Feast of Unleavened Bread, a holy convocation unto us, a memorial of the departure from Egypt. Thou hast chosen us for Thy service and hast made us sharers in the blessings of Thy holy festivals. Blessed art Thou, O Lord, who sanctifiest Israel and the festive seasons.

All read in unison:

Praised art Thou, O Lord our God, Ruler of the world, who hast created the fruit of the vine.

Drink the first cup of wine.

Some parsley, lettuce or watercress is distributed to all present who dip it in salt water or in vinegar, and before partaking of it say in unison:

Praised art Thou, O Lord our God, King of the universe, Creator of the fruit of the earth.

The leader breaks the middle Matzo, *leaving one half on the Seder-dish, and hiding the other half as the* Aphikomon *to be eaten at the end of the meal.*

The leader lifts up the Matzos *and says:*

Lo! This is the bread of affliction which our fathers ate in the land of Egypt. Let all who are hungry come and eat. Let all who are in want come

and celebrate the Passover with us. May it be God's will to redeem us from all trouble and from all servitude. Next year at this season, may the whole house of Israel be free!

The leader replaces the dish upon the table.

The Four Questions

The youngest person at the table asks:

1. Why is this night different from all other nights? On all other nights, we eat either leavened or unleavened bread. Why, on this night, do we eat only unleavened bread?

2. On all other nights, we eat all kinds of herbs. Why, on this night, do we eat especially bitter herbs?

3. On all other nights, we do not dip herbs in any condiment. Why, on this night, do we dip them in salt water and *haroses?*

4. On all other nights, we eat without special festivities. Why, on this night, do we hold this Seder service?

The leader answers:

We celebrate tonight because we were Pharaoh's bondmen in Egypt, and the Lord our God delivered us with a mighty hand. Had not the Holy One, blessed be He, redeemed our fathers from Egypt, we, our children, and our children's children would have remained slaves. Therefore even if all of us were wise and well-versed in the Torah, it would still be our duty from year to year, to tell the story of the deliverance from Egypt. Indeed to dwell at length on it, is accounted praiseworthy.

The Four Sons

By a fitting answer to the questions of each of the four types of the sons of Israel, does the Torah explain the making of this night's celebration.

The wise son eager to learn asks earnestly: "What mean the testimonies and the statutes and the ordinances, which the Lord our God hath commanded us?" To him thou shalt say: "This service is held in order to worship the Lord our God, that it may be well with us all the days of our life."

The wicked son inquires in a mocking spirit: "What mean YE by this service?" As he says YE and not WE, he excludes himself from the household of Israel. Therefore thou shouldst turn on him and say: "It is because of that which the Lord did for ME when I came forth out of Egypt." For ME and not for HIM, for had he been there, he would not have been found worthy of being redeemed.

The simple son indifferently asks: "What is this?"

To him thou shalt say: "By strength of hand the Lord brought us out of Egypt, out of the house of bondage."

And for the son who is unable to inquire, thou shalt explain the whole story of the Passover; as it is said: "And thou shalt tell thy son in that day, saying, 'It is because of that which the Lord did for me when I came forth out of Egypt.'"

The Story of the Oppression

It is well for all of us whether young or old to consider how God's help has been our unfailing stay and support through ages of trial and persecution. Ever since He called our father Abraham from the bondage of idolatry to His service of truth, He has been our Guardian; for not in one country alone nor in one age have violent men risen up against us, but in every generation and in every land, tyrants have sought to destroy us; and the Holy One, blessed be He, has delivered us from their hands.

And Joseph died, and all his brethren, and all that generation. Now there arose a new king over Egypt, who knew not Joseph. And he said unto his people: "Behold, the people of the children of Israel are too many and too mighty for us; come, let us

deal wisely with them, lest they multiply, and it come to pass, that when there befalleth us any war, they also join themselves unto our enemies, and fight against us, and get them up out of the land." Therefore they set over them taskmasters to afflict them with burdens. And they built for Pharaoh store-cities, Pithom and Raamses. But the more the Egyptians afflicted them, the more the Israelites multiplied and the more they spread abroad.

And the Egyptians dealt ill with us, and afflicted us, and laid upon us cruel bondage. And we cried unto the Lord, the God of our fathers, and the Lord heard our voice and saw our affliction and our toil and our oppression. And the Lord brought us forth out of Egypt, with a mighty hand and with an outstretched arm and with great terror and with signs and with wonders. He sent before us Moses and Aaron and Miriam. And He brought forth His people with joy, His chosen ones with singing. And He guided them in the wilderness, as a shepherd his flock.

Therefore He commanded us to observe the Passover in its season, from year to year, that His law shall be in our mouths, and that we shall declare His might unto our children, His salvation to all generations.

All read in unison:

Who is like unto Thee, O Lord, among the mighty?

Who is like unto Thee, glorious in holiness,

Fearful in praises, doing wonders?
The Lord shall reign forever and ever.

Dayenu

The company repeats the refrain Dayenu *which is
equivalent to "It would have satisfied us."*

How manifold are the favors which God has conferred upon us!

Had He brought us out of Egypt, and not divided the sea for us, *Dayenu!*

Had He divided the sea, and not permitted us to cross on dry land, *Dayenu!*

Had He permitted us to cross the sea on dry land, and not sustained us for forty years in the desert, *Dayenu!*

Had He sustained us for forty years in the desert, and not fed us with manna, *Dayenu!*

Had He fed us with manna, and not ordained the Sabbath, *Dayenu!*

Had He ordained the Sabbath, and not brought us to Mount Sinai, *Dayenu!*

Had He brought us to Mount Sinai, and not given us the Torah, *Dayenu!*

Had He given us the Torah, and not led us into the Land of Israel, *Dayenu!*

Had He led us into the Land of Israel, and not built for us the Temple, *Dayenu!*

Had He built for us the Temple, and not sent us prophets of truth, *Dayenu!*

Had He sent us prophets of truth, and not made us a holy people, *Dayenu!*

All read in unison:

How much more then are we to be grateful unto the Lord for the manifold favors which He has bestowed upon us! He brought us out of Egypt, divided the Red Sea for us, permitted us to cross on dry land, sustained us for forty years in the desert, fed us with manna, ordained the Sabbath, brought us to Mount Sinai, gave us the Torah, led us into the Land of Israel, built for us the Temple, sent unto us prophets of truth, and made us a holy people to perfect the world under the kingdom of the Almighty, in truth and in righteousness.

The Passover Symbols

Should enemies again assail us, the remembrance of the exodus of our fathers from Egypt will never fail to inspire us with new courage, and the symbols of this festival will help to strengthen our faith in God, who redeems the oppressed.

Therefore, Rabban Gamaliel, a noted sage, declared: "Whoever does not well consider the meaning of these three symbols: *Pesah, Matzo,* and *Moror,* has not truly celebrated this Festival."

PESAH

One of the company asks:

What is the meaning of *Pesah?*

The leader lifts up the roasted shank-bone and answers:

Pesah means the PASCHAL LAMB, and is symbolized by this shank-bone. It was eaten by our fathers while the Temple was in existence, as a memorial of God's favors, as it is said: "It is the sacrifice of the Lord's PASSOVER, for that He PASSED OVER the houses of the children of Israel in Egypt, when He

smote the Egyptians and delivered our houses." As God in the ancient "Watch-Night" passed over and spared the houses of Israel, so did He save us in all kinds of distress, and so may He always shield the afflicted, and forever remove every trace of bondage from among the children of man.

MATZO

One of the company asks:

What is the meaning of *Matzo?*

The leader lifts up the Matzo *and answers:*

Matzo, called THE BREAD OF AFFLICTION, was the hasty provision that our fathers made for their journey, as it is said: "And they baked unleavened cakes of the dough which they brought out of Egypt. There was not sufficient time to leaven it, for they were driven out of Egypt and could not tarry, neither had they prepared for themselves any provisions. "The bread which of necessity they baked unleavened, thus became a symbol of divine help.

MOROR

One of the company asks:

And what is the meaning of *Moror?*

The leader lifts up the bitter herbs and answers:

Moror means BITTER HERB. We eat it in order to recall that the lives of our ancestors were embit-

tered by the Egyptians, as we read: "And they made their lives bitter with hard labor in mortar and bricks and in all manner of field labor. Whatever task was imposed upon them, was executed with the utmost rigor." As we eat it in the midst of the festivities of this night, we rejoice in the heroic spirit which trials developed in our people. Instead of becoming embittered by them, they were sustained and strengthened.

The Watch-Night of the Eternal

In every generation, each Jew should regard himself as though he too were brought out of Egypt. Not our fathers alone, but us also, did the Holy One redeem; for not alone in Egypt but in many other lands, have we groaned under the burden of affliction and suffered as victims of malice, ignorance and fanaticism. This very night, which we, a happy generation, celebrate so calmly and safely and joyfully in our habitations was often turned into a night of anxiety and of suffering for our people in former times. Cruel mobs were ready to rush upon them and to destroy their homes and the fruit of their labors. But undauntedly they clung to their faith in the ultimate triumph of right and of freedom. Champions of God, they marched from one Egypt into another—driven in haste, their property a prey to the rapacious foe, with their bundles on their shoulders, and God in their hearts.

Because God, "the Guardian of Israel, who sleepeth not nor slumbereth" revealed Himself on that WATCH-NIGHT IN EGYPT and in all dark periods of our past, as the Redeemer of the enslaved, we keep this as a WATCH-NIGHT FOR ALL THE CHILDREN OF ISRAEL, dedicated to God our redeemer.

While enjoying the liberty of this land, let us strive to make secure also our spiritual freedom, that, as the delivered, we may become the deliverer, carrying out Israel's historic task of being the messenger of religion unto all mankind.

All read in unison:

So it is our duty to thank, praise and glorify God, who brought us and our forefathers from slavery unto freedom, from sorrow unto joy, from mourning unto festive gladness, from darkness unto light. Let us therefore proclaim His praise.

Hallel

Psalm 113

Leader:

Hallelujah.
Praise, O ye servants of the Lord,
Praise the name of the Lord.

Company:

Blessed be the name of the Lord
From this time forth and forever.

Leader:

From the rising of the sun unto the going down
    thereof
The Lord's name is to be praised.

Company:

The Lord is high above all nations,
His glory is above the heavens.

Leader:

Who is like unto the Lord our God,
That is enthroned on high,

Company:

That looketh down low
Upon heaven and upon earth?

Leader:

Who raiseth up the poor out of the dust,
And lifteth up the needy out of the dunghill;

Company:

That He may set him with princes,
Even with the princes of His people.

Leader:

Who maketh the barren woman to dwell in her
　　house
As a joyful mother of children.

Company:

Hallelujah.

PSALM 114

Leader:

When Israel came forth out of Egypt,
The house of Jacob from a people of strange
　　language;

Company:

Judah became His sanctuary,
Israel His dominion.

Leader:

The sea saw it, and fled;
The Jordan turned backward.

Company:

The mountains skipped like rams,
The hills like young sheep.

Leader:

What aileth thee, O thou sea, that thou fleest?
Thou Jordan, that thou turnest backward?

Company:

Ye mountains that ye skip like rams;
Ye hills, like young sheep?

Leader:

Tremble, thou earth, at the presence of the lord,
At the presence of the God of Jacob;

Company:

Who turned the rock into a pool of water,
The flint into a fountain of waters.

Blessings

Praised art Thou, O Lord our God, King of the universe, who hast redeemed us and our ancestors from Egypt, and hast enabled us to observe this night of the Passover, the Feast of Unleavened Bread. O Lord our God and God of our fathers, may we, with Thy help, live to celebrate other feasts and holy seasons. May we rejoice in Thy salvation and be gladdened by Thy righteousness. Grant deliverance to mankind through Israel, Thy people. May Thy will be done through Jacob, Thy chosen servant, so that Thy name shall be sanctified in the midst of all the earth, and that all peoples be moved to worship Thee with one accord. And we shall sing new songs of praise unto Thee, for our redemption and for the deliverance of our souls. Praised art Thou, O God, Redeemer of Israel.

The cups are filled for the second time.

All read in unison:

Praised art Thou, O Lord our God, King of the universe, who hast created the fruit of the vine.

Drink the second cup of wine.

The upper Matzo is broken and distributed. All then read in unison:

Praised art Thou, O Lord our God, King of the universe, who bringest forth bread from the earth.

Praised art Thou, O Lord our God, King of the universe, who hast sanctified us through Thy commandments, and ordained that we should eat unleavened bread.

Eat the Matzo.

Each person receives some bitter herbs and haroses, which he places between two pieces of matzo. *The leader then reads:*

This was the practice of Hillel, at the time the Temple was still in existence. He combined the unleavened bread and the bitter herbs and ate them together, to carry out the injunction concerning the Passover sacrifice: "With unleavened bread and with bitter herbs, they shall eat it."

All read in unison:

Praised art Thou, O Lord our God, King of the universe, who hast sanctified us by Thy commandments, and ordained that we should eat bitter herbs.

Eat the Moror.

SUPPER IS THEN SERVED

Partake of the Aphikomon.

At the conclusion of the meal, the children are given an opportunity to find the Aphikomon. *The reader redeems it and distributes pieces of it to all present.*

After partaking of the Aphikomon, *it is customary to eat nothing else.*

Grace after the Meal

Leader:

Let us say grace.

Company:

Let us bless Him of whose bounty we have partaken and through whose goodness we live.

Leader:

Praised art Thou, O Lord our God, King of the universe, who sustainest the world with goodness, with grace, and with infinite mercy. Thou givest food unto every creature, for Thy mercy endureth forever.

Company:

Through Thy great goodness, food has not failed

us. May it never fail us at any time, for the sake of Thy great name.

Leader:

Thou sustainest and dealest graciously with all Thy creatures.

Company:

Praised art Thou, O Lord, who givest food unto all.

All read in unison:

O God, our Father, sustain and protect us and grant us strength to bear our burdens. Let us not, O God, become dependent upon men, but let us rather depend upon Thy hand, which is ever open and gracious, so that we may never be put to shame.

Leader:

God and God of our fathers, be Thou ever mindful of us, as Thou hast been of our fathers, so that we may find enlargement, grace, mercy, life and peace on this Feast of Unleavened Bread.

Company: AMEN

Remember us this day in kindness.

Company: AMEN

Visit us this day with blessing.

Company: AMEN

Preserve us this day for life.

Company: AMEN

With Thy saving and gracious word have mercy

upon us and save us, for unto Thee, the compassionate and merciful One, our eyes are ever turned, for Thou art a gracious and merciful King.

The All-merciful! May He reign over us forever!

Company: AMEN

The All-merciful! May He sustain us in honor!

Company: AMEN

The All-merciful! May He bless this household and all assembled here. May we all find favor in the eyes of God and men!

Company: AMEN

Leader:

Fear ye the Lord, ye His holy ones, for there is no want to them that fear Him.

Company:

The young lions do lack and suffer hunger, but they that seek the Lord shall not lack any good thing.

Leader:

O give thanks unto the Lord, for He is good, for His mercy endureth forever.

Company:

Thou openest Thy hand and satisfiest every living thing with favor.

Leader:

Blessed is the man that trusteth in the Lord; the Lord shall be unto him for a help.

Company:

The Lord will give strength unto His people;
The Lord will bless His people with peace.

The cups are filled for the third time.

All read in unison:

Blessed art Thou, O Lord our God, King of the universe, who createst the fruit of the vine.

Drink the third cup of wine.

THE DOOR IS OPENED FOR ELIJAH

PSALM 117

Leader:

Praise the Lord, all ye nations;

Company:

Laud Him, all ye peoples.

Leader:

For His mercy is great toward us;

Company:

And the truth of the Lord endureth forever. Hallelujah!

THE DOOR IS CLOSED.

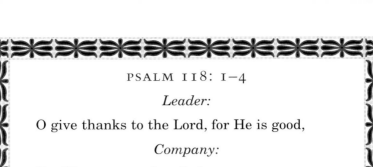

PSALM 118: 1–4

Leader:

O give thanks to the Lord, for He is good,

Company:

For His mercy endureth forever.

Leader:

So let Israel now say,

Company:

For His mercy endureth forever.

Leader:

So let the house of Aaron now say,

Company:

For His mercy endureth forever.

Leader:

So let them now that fear the Lord say,

Company:

For His mercy endureth forever.

PSALM 118: 5–29

Leader:

Out of distress I called upon the Lord;
He answered me with great enlargement.

Company:

The Lord is for me; I will not fear; what can man do unto me?

Leader:

It is better to take refuge in the Lord than to trust in man.

Company:

It is better to take refuge in the Lord than to trust in princes.

Leader:

The Lord is my strength and song; and He is become my salvation.

Company:

The voice of rejoicing and salvation is in the tents of the righteous.

Leader:

The right hand of the Lord doeth valiantly; the right hand of the Lord is exalted.

Company:

I shall not die but live, and declare the works of the Lord.

Leader:

The Lord hath chastened me sore; but He hath not given me over unto death.

Company:

Open to me the gates of righteousness; I will enter into them; I will give thanks unto the Lord.

Leader:

This is the gate of the Lord; the righteous shall enter into it.

Company:

I will give thanks unto Thee, for Thou hast answered me, and art become my salvation.

Leader:

The stone which the builders rejected is become the chief cornerstone.

Company:

This is the Lord's doing; it is marvelous in our eyes.

Leader:

This is the day which the Lord hath made; we will rejoice and be glad in it.

Company:

We beseech Thee, O Lord, save now! We beseech Thee, O Lord, make us now to prosper!

Leader:

Blessed be he that cometh in the name of the Lord;

Company:

We bless you out of the house of the Lord.

Leader:

Thou art my God, and I will give thanks unto Thee;

Company:

Thou art my God, I will exalt Thee.

Leader:

O give thanks unto the Lord, for He is good,

Company:

For His mercy endureth forever.

The Final Benediction

The cups are filled for the fourth time.

The leader lifts the cup of wine and reads:

The festive service is completed. With songs of praise, we have lifted up the cups symbolizing the divine promise of salvation, and have called upon the name of God. As we offer the Benediction over the fourth cup, let us again lift our souls to God in faith and in hope. May He who broke Pharaoh's yoke forever shatter all fetters of oppression, and

hasten the day when swords shall, at last, be broken and wars ended. Soon may He cause the glad tidings of redemption to be heard in all lands, so that mankind—freed from violence and from wrong, and united in an eternal covenant of brotherhood—may celebrate the universal Passover in the name of our God of freedom.

All read in unison:

May God bless the whole house of Israel with freedom, and keep us safe from danger everywhere. Amen.

May God cause the light of His countenance to shine upon all men, and dispel the darkness of ignorance and of prejudice. May He be gracious unto us.

Amen. May God lift up His countenance upon our country and render it a true home of liberty and a bulwark of justice. And may He grant peace unto us and unto all mankind. Amen.

Praised art Thou, O Lord our God, King of the universe, who createst the fruit of the vine.

Drink the fourth cup of wine.

Passover Recipes

Chicken Soup with Matzo Balls

Known to the world over as "Jewish Penicillin," chicken soup is acclaimed for its wondrous curative as well as gustatory powers. This recipe can be varied with the seasons and to the taste of the cook. Makes about 12 servings.

SOUP:

- 12 *cups water*
- 1 *large, clean soup chicken with gizzard and neck*
- 3 *stalks of celery, cleaned and cut into $\frac{1}{4}$-inch pieces*
- 2 *onions, halved*
- 4 *carrots, cleaned and cut into $\frac{1}{2}$-inch pieces dill*
- $\frac{1}{2}$ *teaspoon garlic*
- 6 *peppercorns*
- 2 *tablespoons salt*
- $\frac{1}{2}$ *teaspoon nutmeg bunch of fresh parsley or 2 tablespoons dry parsley*

MATZO BALLS:

- 5 *eggs*
- $\frac{1}{2}$ *teaspoon salt*
- $\frac{1}{2}$ *teaspoon pepper matzo meal*

Bring water and ingredients to a boil in a pot, then turn flame down to a simmer. Cook chicken for about 2 or 3 hours, or until it is tender. Then remove chicken and bone it, throwing out fat, skin, and bones. Put chicken meat into soup and refrigerate. After it has cooled, remove congealed fat to use for matzo balls. Mix fat with beaten eggs, salt, pepper, and matzo meal to make a loose dough (approximately $1\frac{1}{2}$ to 2 cups). Refrigerate matzo mixture, covered, for at about 2 hours or more, until the loose dough becomes firm. To serve, about an hour before dinner, heat soup to a boil. Form matzo mixture into 1-inch balls and put them all into the pot with the soup, covering immediately and turning flame down to a simmer. Cook for about 45 minutes to 1 hour more.

Gefilte Fish

Among Eastern-European Jews, gefilte fish is a traditional fish appetizer served on Passover. This recipe makes about 60 pieces of fish.

STOCK:

> fish bones, heads, divided between two 10–12 quart pots
> 3 quarts water in each of two pots
> 8 carrots, sliced, divided between two pots
> 1 celery root, cleaned and divided between two pots

    2 *large onions, sliced, divided between two pots*
  1½ *tablespoons salt in each of two pots*
  1½ *tablespoons black or white pepper in each of*
       two pots

FISH:

    7 *pounds, boneless and skinless filets of cod*
       (use bones and heads in stock)
    3 *pounds, boneless and skinless filets of salmon*
       (use bones and heads in stock)
    2 *very large onions*
  1½ *cups matzo meal*
    4 *carrots*
    1 *cup water*
  1–2 *tablespoons white or black pepper*
    2 *tablespoons salt*
    8 *eggs*
   ½ *cup olive oil*

To make stock, put all stock ingredients in the two pots, and bring to a boil. Simmer, covered, at low heat, and meanwhile prepare the fish.

Use a food processor to grind the fish, then the onions (very fine), matzo meal, and carrots. Then put all ingredients, in the order they are ground, into a large tub. Beat water, pepper, salt, eggs and oil in the food processor until it has a mousse-like consistency. Then add this into the fish mixture in the tub and mix thoroughly.

Form ½ to 1 cup of mixture into balls, and place, with care, into the simmering stock. Distribute the fish equally in the two pots, and simmer, covered for

$1\frac{1}{2}$ hours. Then let cool for a while, before removing fish and vegetables to storage containers. Strain the liquid over the fish and remove the pieces of carrots and onions and put with the fish. Throw away the bones. Then store the fish well refrigerated. At Seder, serve with mild or hot prepared horseradish.

Root Vegetable Kugel

1–2 *large carrots, peeled*
1 *medium turnip, peeled and quartered*
1 *large white potato, peeled and quartered*
1 *large sweet potato, peeled and quartered*
1 *small onion, peeled*
2 *eggs*
2 *tablespoons matzo meal*
$\frac{1}{2}$ *teaspoon salt*
$\frac{1}{2}$ *teaspoon pepper*
$\frac{1}{2}$ *teaspoon dried sage leaves*
$\frac{1}{2}$ *teaspoon dried thyme*
$\frac{1}{4}$ *cup melted margarine or oil*

Chop all vegetables in a food processor and add remaining ingredients, mixing for about 30 seconds. In a greased cake pan or casserole, bake at 350°F. for about $1\frac{1}{4}$ hours. Makes about 6 servings.

Vegetable Cutlets

      3 *teaspoons olive oil*
      1 *chopped green pepper*
      1 *large onion, chopped*
      2 *cups chopped carrots*
      3 *tablespoons chopped parsley*
     10 *ounces chopped spinach (fresh or frozen)*
      3 *eggs, beaten*
$1\frac{1}{2}$ *teaspoons salt*
 $\frac{1}{2}$ *teaspoon pepper*
 $\frac{3}{4}$ *cup matzo meal*
         additional olive oil for frying

Sauté green pepper, onion, parsley, and carrot in oil for 5 minutes. Cook spinach and drain. Combine all vegetables and add eggs, salt, pepper, and matzo meal. Drop into hot oil by large spoonfuls and brown well. Makes 12–15 cutlets.

Chocolate Cake for Passover

     10 *eggs, separated, at room temperature*
     14 *tablespoons sugar*
      6 *ounces bittersweet chocolate, melted*
      2 *cups nuts, finely chopped*

Preheat oven to 350°F. Beat egg yolks and sugar until very thick and lemon colored, at which point, stir in the chocolate, then fold in the nuts. Beat egg whites until stiff—but not dry—and fold into the mixture. Pour mixture into a greased 10 inch spring form pan. Bake for about 1 hour or when the center of the cake springs back when lightly touched. Allow to cool in the pan. Makes about 10 servings.

Coconut Macaroons

These simple cookies are a Passover favorite and are a treat any time of the year. Makes about 30–40 cookies.

> 3 *large egg whites*
> $5\frac{1}{3}$ *cups sweetened flake coconut*
> $\frac{1}{2}$ *cup granulated sugar*
> $\frac{1}{4}$ *teaspoon pure vanilla extract*

Preheat oven to 300°F. Beat the egg whites until stiff and fold in all the ingredients with a large rubber scraper. Drop $\frac{1}{2}$-inch spoonfuls onto foil-lined cookie sheets, separated by about 1 inch. Bake for 15 minutes.